When Jack Sued Jill

Nursery Rhymes
for Modern Times

Acclaim for Felix Dennis
'Lone Wolf' and *'A Glass Half Full'*

"He writes like a man obsessed... if Waugh were still alive, he would fall on Dennis's verse with a glad cry of recognition and approval."
— **John Walsh,** *The Independent*

"Marvellous stuff... the unpredictable Felix Dennis, long known for publishing other things, now bursts forth as a 21st century Kipling."
— **Tom Wolfe,** critic and author

"Seriously good... great quality and memorability. At least one of these poems will be instantly anthologised."
— **Melvyn Bragg,** broadcaster and author

"Witty, thought provoking and moving. You may even cry! I loved it."
— **Dave Reynolds,** Radio Warwick

"I enjoyed *A Glass Half Full* more than I can possibly say. Brilliant!"
— **Helen Gurley Brown,** International Editor in Chief, *Cosmopolitan*

"A fantastic collection. Rich, sumptuous and beautifully threaded."
— **Jon Snow,** Channel 4 broadcaster

"I don't know which is better— hearing him read them aloud or reading the book itself."
— **Dotun Adebayo,** BBC Radio London

"Felix is a pirate and a passionate poet... an evening to remember."
— **Michael Boyd,** Artistic Director, Royal Shakespeare Company

"I enjoy his poetry immensely..."
— **Mick Jagger,** The Rolling Stones

"Many people were deeply moved by the humanity of his verse and by the range of his experience [in these] haunting poems."
— **Tom Wujec,** TED Conference Monterey, California

"He's a magazine publisher by accident. He's a poet, a pirate and he does whatever he wants. He's a joy to have as a British person."
— **Chris Hughes,** Publishing Director, *Good Housekeeping*

ACC. No: 02593484

By the same author:

Muhammad Ali: The Glory Years
(with Don Atyeo)

A Glass Half Full

Lone Wolf

How To Get Rich

When Jack Sued Jill

Nursery Rhymes for Modern Times

Felix Dennis

Illustrated by
Bill Sanderson & Sebastian Krüger

Designed and coloured by
Mike Dunn

First published in Great Britain 2006

3 5 7 9 10 8 6 4 2

© Felix Dennis 2006

Ebury Press, an imprint of Ebury Publishing.
Random House, 20 Vauxhall Bridge Road, London SW1V 2SA

Random House Australia (Pty) Limited
20 Alfred Street, Milsons Point, Sydney, New South Wales 2061, Australia

Random House New Zealand Limited
18 Poland Road, Glenfield, Auckland 10, New Zealand

Random House (Pty) Limited
Isle of Houghton, Corner of Boundary Road and Carse O'Gowrie,
Houghton, 2198, South Africa

Random House Publishers India Private Limited
301 World Trade Tower, Hotel Intercontinental Grand Complex,
Barakhamba Lane, New Delhi 110 001, India

The Random House Group Limited Reg. No. 954009

www.randomhouse.co.uk

A CIP catalogue record for this book is available from the British Library.

ISBN 9780091912567 (after Jan 2007)
ISBN 0091912563

Papers used by Ebury Press are natural, recyclable products
made from wood grown in sustainable forests.

Set in Clarendon.
Printed and bound in Great Britain by
Butler & Tanner Ltd, Frome and London.

In memory of
Michael Homewood Nixon

Contents

Author's note

There is more than meets the eye to many nursery rhymes and some of them are perhaps far older than modern versions suggest. Was 'Humpty Dumpty' King Richard III or 'Jack Spratt' Charles I? Was 'Baa Baa Black Sheep' a coded complaint about taxation or 'The Old Woman Who Lived in a Shoe' concerned with the perils of empire? 'Ring a Ring a Rosie' is certainly about the plague — but which plague?

Despite a great deal of scholarly research into nursery rhymes, the origins of many of them remain obscure. Perhaps only one thing is certain: their survival and enduring popularity is due as much to their sound as to their content and to the imagery they conjure up rather than to their meaning — if, indeed, they ever *had* a 'meaning'. I've tried to bear that in mind when rewriting them.

The variety of their original subject matter was a particular inspiration. It meant that I felt free to hammer away at whatever (or whoever) had annoyed me in the newspapers that day. In its secret heart, much poetry and song is a hymn of complaint. Man is a universal whinger and whiner, which is why there are so many more memorable laments than odes to joy in almost all cultures.

In this little book, then, I grapple with the niggles and outrages of everyday life in the 21st century: divorce, immigration, political correctness, globalisation, the EU, celebrity culture, ecological cant, pension shortfalls, obesity, educational standards, tabloid journalism, healthcare costs and technology fads.

To a lesser extent I have also wrestled with those staples of human misery — war, famine, genocide, racism, sexual inequality, tyranny, religious fundamentalism and xenophobia. But these, I fear, are less easily reduced to doggerel or rhyme of any kind, not being the petty foibles of a particular age, but the backdrop to the human condition since first we walked upon two legs.

Felix Dennis
Dorsington, Warwickshire 2006

www.felixdennis.com

This Little Piggy

This little piggy was a burglar,
This little piggy was a thief,
This little piggy broke in my house,
This little piggy came to grief,
This little piggy squealed *'Wee, wee, wee, wee, wee!*

You walloped me and now I'll claim relief!
A modern thief in no way is naïf!
My legal aid will buy a fancy brief!
And then I'm off to live in Tenerife!'

Anti-Social Behaviour Orders

[To the tune of 'Twinkle, Twinkle Little Star']

ASBO, ASBO, little law,
How we wonder what you're for,
Chavs and yobs who love to fight
Terrorise us every night.
Toothless, useless, little law,
How we wonder what you're for.

On the streets with hoods and knives,
How they terrorise our lives,
Though they all should be in bed,
All you do is boost their cred'.
ASBO, ASBO, can't you see
You are an accessory.

ASBO, ASBO, little law,
How we wonder what you're for,
Words will never rule the street,
We need coppers on the beat.
Toothless, useless, little law,
How we wonder what you're for.

These Old Men

[Knick Knack Paddy Whack]

Jacques Chirac, he played one,
Grumpy voters spoiled his fun,
With a knick knack paddy whack,
Give the Frog a bone,
This old man came limping home.

Gerhard S, he played two,
April's Child bids you adieu,
With a knick knack paddy whack,
Give the Kraut a bob,
This old man has lost his job.

Tony Blair, he played three,
Posing now as Mrs. T,
With a knick knack paddy whack,
Give the Brit a spin,
This old man has lost his grin.

Silvio B, he played four,
Wise-guys waiting at the door,
With a knick knack paddy whack,
Give the Don a pail,
This old man is off to jail.

These old men, they played five,
How they love to duck and dive,
With a knick knack paddy whack,
Give 'em all away,
These old dogs have had their day.

'Boys and girls come out to play...'

Boys and girls come out to play,
The team is playing away today,
We're off to shake the Germans up,
Nobody cares if we win the cup,
We planned it all on the internet,
Techno-Yobs-R-Us, you bet,
Up the ladder and down the wall,
We'll put the lot in the hospital,
Break a bottle and choose a Kraut,
The bastards all need sorting out,
Bring your mates to join the fight,
And be on the TV news tonight.

There Was a Crooked Man

(The Enron Song)

There was a crooked man,
    And he had a crooked smile,
He bought a crooked company,
To make a crooked pile,
He bribed a crooked crony
To form a crooked Board,
And all its regulations
Were crookedly ignored,
He paid a crooked banker,
To rig a crooked sale,
And they all lived together
In a crooked little gaol.

'People of Colour'

'*People of Colour*'?
        A brave accolade,
  And the last two words so much hullabaloo.
Has pink now ceased to count as a shade,
  Or am I not 'people' to such as you?

'*People of Colour*'!
        You wretched Uriah!
  What's bred in the bone is a rainbow quilt,
Enemy— friend— belovéd— pariah,
  A man is a *man*, not a palette of guilt.

'Georgie Porgie...'

Georgie Porgie,
      pudding and pie,
Kissed the girls
      and made them cry,
When teacher heard
      what he had done
She made him put
      a condom on.

Georgie Porgie,
      bully and clown,
His hands are damp,
      his nose is brown,
He scraped through
      university,
And now it's
      Georgie P. M.P!

'Allah Akbar!'

The Semtex strapped around him,
　　His heart devoid of fear,
'Allah Akbar! God is Great!
　　And paradise stands near.
　　I wreak His vengeance here!'

A schoolboy kicks his classmate,
　　The blow repaid in kind.
'Eye for an eye' we teach them,
　　And one day— shall we find
　　All humankind gone blind?

Baa, Baa, Aids Sheep

Baa, Baa, Aids sheep
   Have you any pills?
No, sir, no, sir,
   None for my ills;
None for my symptoms,
   And none 'til I die,
The company that makes them
   Charges way too high.

Four is the Number

[A nursery rhyme for Creationists]

A is to T as C is to G,
T is to G as A is to C,
G is to A as C is to T,
Four is the number from zebra to bee.

G is to A as C is to T,
A is to T as C is to G,
T is to G as A is to C,
Four is the number from monkey to flea.

T is to G as A is to C,
G is to A as C is to T,
A is to T as C is to G,
Four is the number from turtle to tree.

A is to T as C is to G,
T is to G as A is to C,
G is to A as C is to T,
Four is the number from Adam to thee...

...and you, and me, and you, and me!

All life on our planet is connected. We know this now beyond all doubt. Perhaps, in our heart of hearts, we always knew it. For religious fundementalists, however, the discovery of the structure of DNA must have splashed beside them like a lifeline from a ship in the Devil's navy. Here is the strongest 'proof' yet of the eternal 'Watchmaker' whose universal design received such a battering from the disciples of Darwin. Yet is the discovery of the structure of DNA and of the four chemical letters scientists designate A,T,G and C, (the basis of all life's hereditary characteristics), a noose or a reef knot? Human DNA is 99% the same as that of a chimpanzee. This proof of our common ancestry may well have as great an impact on religious philosophy, in the long run, as it already has had, and will continue to have, among the scientists who man Old Nick's Armada.

Ol' Man Sorrow

Ol' Man Sorrow got a sack
Heavy 'nuff to break yo' back,

When you meet him on de road
Nebber, nebber share dat load,

Nod: "G'mornin", sidle by,
Cross yo'self and hope to die,

If he walk on — den you run!
Jumbie bad— he go to come!

Iffen he chase af'er you,
Get yo'self to Timbuktu,

Sell yo' shoes and pawn yo' coat,
Smuggle yo'self 'board a boat,

If he wait dere on de deck,
Tie de millstone roun' yo' neck,

Jump into de sea below —
Dat one place he *nebber* go.

Ol' Man Sorrow got a sack
Heavy 'nuff to break yo' back.

When sorrows come, they come not single spies, / But in battalions.' (Hamlet act 4, sc 5.) In the West Indies, they come in a sack. Several of the lines from this sly nursery rhyme came from a group of Caribbean fisherman over a 'boil-up' and cups of rum around the fire in their fishing village. Political correctness probably demands that 'de' be spelt as 'the'; 'yo' be spelt 'your' and 'nebber' be spelt 'never' etc. But as my pc rating is zero, I have spelt them as they are spoken in that part of the world. A 'jumbie' is an evil spirit or bogey man.

Hacker-boy, hacker-boy

[Pussycat, Pussycat, Where Have You Been?]

Hacker-boy, hacker-boy, where have you been?
I sat in my bedroom and stared at a screen.
Hacker-boy, hacker-boy, what did you see?
I built a new virus upon my PC.

Hacker-boy, hacker-boy, where is it now?
It is shutting the lights off in Rome and Macao.
Hacker-boy, hacker-boy, what did you do?
I proved that I'm better than anyone knew.

Hacker-boy, hacker boy, why do you smile?
My virus has wormed through a Pentagon file.
Hacker-boy, hacker-boy, why are you sad?
They've put me in prison for being so bad.

'Hey diddle diddle...'

Hey diddle diddle,
I've punctured my middle
And stapled a ring in my nose;
My thingummy's lips
Are pierced at the tips
And I jingles wherever I goes!

Humpty Dumpty

Humpty Dumpty snorted some coke,
Humpty Dumpty poisoned his yolk,
All the Do-gooders and all the King's Men
Kept putting Humpty in rehab again.

Humpty Dumpty shot up some smack,
Humpty Dumpty fell on his back,
All the Probational Officer's men
Never put Humpty together again.

'Oranges and Lemons...'

Oranges and lemons
　Say the bells of the Netherlands,

You owe me my subsidy,
Say the bells of South Italy.

Why aren't we rich?
Say the bells of Maastrich.

Where has it gone?
Say the bells of Lisbon.

France took it all,
Say the bells of St. Paul.

Zat is a libel!
Say the bells on the Eiffel.

Who'll pay the fine?
Say the bells on the Rhine.

It must be you,
Say the bells of EU.

It won't be us!
Say the bells in chorus.

Here come a summit to spin all the facts.
Here comes a whopping great increase in tax.

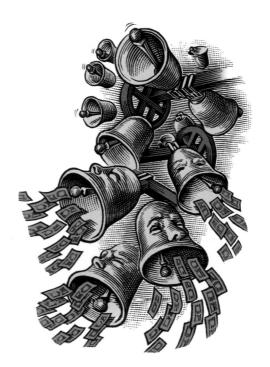

'Sing a song of sixpence...'

'Sing a song of sixpence,
   A pocket full of rye;
Four and twenty blackbirds,
   Baked in a pie'.

Let me see your sixpence,
   What a pretty piece;
The Trading Standards Officer
   Is calling the police.

Open up your microwave,
   What have you to say?
Scoffing pretty songbirds,
   Lock the brute away.

Do not call them blackbirds,
   You racist balladeers;
Stirring ethnic hatred —
   Four and twenty years!

What's Good for the Goose

If every father, son and daughter
Went to match their DNA,
My word, there'd be an awful slaughter,
Like as not with little quarter,
If those daddies ever caught the
Mummies who'd been making hay!

How Many Miles to Babylon?

How many miles to Babylon?
Three score miles and ten.
Can I get there by candlelight?
Yes, and back again.

Will going void my Warranty?
Tick the box below.
May I bring a friend with me?
Neither friend nor foe.

How many clicks to Paradise?
Tech support will know.
Is software there compatible?
Check before you go.

How many souls to fill the Pit?
As many as are men.
How many chances do I get?
Game over. Play again?

Jack and Jill

Jack and Jill went up the hill
   To fetch a pail of water;
  Jack fell down and broke his crown
And Jill came tumbling after.

Jill sued Jack and Jack sued back,
  The judge is going to fine her;
Now the pail's been sent to jail
  For abandoning a minor.

We'll sue Jack and he'll sue Jill,
  The hill is suing for scandal;
The water says he'll sue the press—
  And everyone's suing the handle.

'Headless Corpse...'
[Ode to The Sun]

Headless Corpse in Topless Bar;
Fog Descends on Channel;
My, what wags those editors are:
Get Back On Yer Camel!

Gotcha! — watch those Argie's float,
Drowning while they're waving.
Madman Bites Out Puppy's Throat;
Some Scum Aren't Worth Saving.

Wacko Jacko! Child Molesters!
Vladimir the Vandal!
Red Ken Runs From Zen Protesters;
It's A Bloody Scandal!

Type as black as Satan's hearths;
Gazza's Getting Knotted!
World Exclusive Photographs!
Cambridge Rapist Spotted!

Up Yours Delors! — you naughty *Sun*;
Princess Di's Last Meal;
Name And Shame 'Em, Every One!
Are Pamela's New Tits Real?

Our Readers Have The Right To Know;
Blimey! What A Scorcher!
If You Love Your Country, Go!
Dub'ya — Stop This Torture!

All the headline above came from tabloid newspapers, with the exception of the second, an apocryphal headline supposedly from *The Times* at turn of the last century, which read in full: 'Fog Descends on Channel, Continent Cut Off'. Splendid!

'Cry, baby bunting...'

Bye, baby bunting,
Daddy can't go hunting,
Horse and hound are put away,
Idle spite has won the day.

Cry, baby bunting,
Daddy can't go hunting;
Not a chicken in the pot,
Foxes came and ate the lot.

White Van Man

[To the tune of Old King Cole]

White Van Man has a very white van
    And a very white van has he,
Except for the dents and the rust by the vents
    And some very rude Graf-ee-teeeee.

He drives in his van as fast as he can
    And he neither hears nor sees,
He clings to his phone like a dog with a bone
    While he steers with one of his kneeeees.

He picks his nose while the tailback grows
    And yacks to his front seat crew,
But a fool so rash as to honk or flash
    Will receive the fingers twooooo.

Oh, White Van Man has a very wide clan
    Who profess no Highway Code,
They'll shunt your rear and yell in your ear
    As they U-turn in the roooooad.

He stamps on his brakes when he overtakes
    As he cuts up you and me,
For White Van Man has a very white van...
    And a very white van has heeeee!

'I looked at a rook...'

I looked at a rook,
He looked at me,
I in my nook,
He in his tree.

He gave such a look
Of scorn and pride,
I shut up my book
And crept inside;

I took from a hook
My gun to kill
That haughty rook,
Who meant me ill;

But just as I took
Most careful aim
He gave me a look
That said: *'For shame!*

Before ye came, long, long ago,
These woods were haunt of rook and crow,
Of badger and fox and doe in flight —
A squirrel could swing from Dale to Bight —
Ye think me rude to thus intrude
Upon thy paltry solitude?
And yet thy gun much ruder is,
For which of us intruder is?'

I looked at the rook,
He looked at me,
I in my nook,
He in his tree;

Back to its hook
Went gun — and, aye,
Back to my nook
Went book and I.

'Three Blind Mice...'

Three blind mice. Three blind mice.
See how they run! See how they run!
They all ran after the scientist,
Who blinded their eyes with a fragrance mist,
They're testing their teeth on their torturer's wrist,
Three blind mice!

'I love the French — the bastards...'

I love the French— the bastards,
I love the French— the swine,
It galls me to admit it,
But how I love their wine...

Their cheeses and their clarets,
The muddle of *Franglais,*
Their weird belief that Elvis
Was Johnny 'Allyday...

Their love of regulations,
Which all are then ignored,
The strikes they call on ferries
When everyone's aboard...

Their grandiose delusion
That what is French is right,
Their rascal politicians
Who rob them day and night...

Their summer-long vacations,
Their bloody-minded cheek,
Their loathing of the English,
Their little fits of pique...

The worship of their bellies,
Their shrugs and *savoire-faire* —
I'd move to France tomorrow
If only they weren't there...

I love Provençe in autumn,
And spring in gay *Paris*,
I love the French— the bastards,
But <u>they</u> do not — love <u>me</u>!

'O dear, what can the matter be...'

O dear, what can the matter be?
 Dear, dear, what can the matter be,
O dear, what can the matter be?
Who has the money to pay?
They promised to pay us, they promised on Monday,
They promised to pay us, they promised on Sunday,
They promised to pay us, perhaps they will one day,
Our pensions have melted away.

O dear, what can the matter be?
Dear, dear, what can the matter be,
O dear, what can the matter be?
Nobody knows where it went.
The government says it has emptied its kitties,
They promise us quangos and countless committees,
Yet here am I dining on tea and McVitie's
And never a penny was sent.

O dear, what can the matter be?
Dear, dear, what can the matter be,
O dear, what can the matter be?
All of us marching to town.
We scrimped and we saved to retire in some leisure,
We're tired of waiting on bureaucrats' pleasure,
We're bringing a noose and we know who to measure,
We're coming to hang Mr. Brown.

Lady's Man, Lady's Man

Lady's man, Lady's man,
Fly away home,
Your wife has divorced you,
Your children have gone.
The judge wants to jail you,
He won't set you free
Until you have paid lots
Of alimony!

Why Did the Jews Kill Jesus, Dad?

Why did the Jews kill Jesus?
　'Cos Jesus was a *Jew!*
A trouble-making rebel,
　And stroppy with it, too.

He argued with his betters
　An' 'ung about with yobs,
Chastisin' money-lenders
　An' lecturin' the nobs.

They didn' take *that* kindly,
　No more they would today,
They fitted him up proper, son,
　An' chucked the key away.

The rabbis called on Pontius
　To seize him to be tried,
An' though old Pilate waffled,
　They 'ad him crucified.

Then one of his disciples,
　(A clever git named Paul),
Created a religion,
　Complete with Popes an' all.

'Course, both the Jews and Hayrabs
　Are Semites to the core;
Their ancestor was Shem, son —
　So when they 'ave a war

It's likely to be *nasty!*
　A *civil* war, d'you see?
Now do yer bloody homework,
　An' let me eat me tea.

Needlework

On being instructed in The Elements of Nonsexist Usage (2000)
that persons who sew for a living are now to be referred to as 'sewers'.
[A march in time to the nursery rhyme: They're changing the guard
at Buckingham Palace]

Oh, what has become of the seamstresses?
  ess eee doubleyoo, eee arr ess!
In the pc handbook here, it says:
  ess eee doubleyoo, eee arr ess!

But still it doesn't spell out for shoo-er,
  ess eee doubleyoo, eee arr ess!
If it rhymes with go-er or rhymes with doo-er.
  ess eee doubleyoo, eee arr ess!

All for a dress!
  What mess!
    God bless!

Johnny

Mummy! Johnny set my hair alight!
Mummy! Johnny super-glued the cat!
Mummy! Johnny got into a fight!
    (*And* he told the teacher she was fat).

Mummy! Johnny covered me in paint!
Mummy! Johnny farted for a bet!
Mummy! Johnny taught us how to faint!
    (*And* he let me share a cigarette).

Mummy! Johnny fell into the pool!
Mummy! Johnny taught me how to float!
Mummy! Johnny got expelled from school!
    (*And* he keeps a ferret in his coat).

Mummy! Johnny bought a new guitar!
Mummy! Johnny's gone and dyed his hair!
Mummy! Johnny kissed me in his car!
    (*And* I let him do it Mum, so there!)

Quota Rota

The Chair is panic stricken:
        "I'm afraid we're in a bind,
We've lost our single parent,
        and the black Vice-chair's resigned.
It's all so disappointing.
        New grants would be a cinch
With a lesbian, an amputee —
        or an Asian (at a pinch).
But better — _so_ much better! —
        we'd clinch the grant in spades
With a Muslim in a wheelchair,
        or an Inuit with AIDS."

If these lines appear cynical, they mock only what warrants mockery beyond my pen. In schools and colleges, in charities and not-for-profit organisations, in the armed forces, councils, unions and government, in quangos, churches, boardrooms, the arts and committees beyond counting, the scourge of political correctness surges on unabated. All that stands between this pernicious folly and the death of meritocracy is... mockery. A powerful tool— but is it powerful enough to withstand a tide bent on drowning the Western world in poisonous folly?

Red Riding Hood

Meets the Tabloid Wolf

A dog may sniff at a bishop,
A cat may look at a king,
But a sad old man
By an ice-cream van?
A very suspicious thing!

MOLESTER LOOSE IN THE HIGH STREET!
A MONSTER UP IN THE DOCK!
For a hack to rise
In an editor's eyes:
Cry *WOLF!* to shepherd the flock.

Red Riding Hood's out walking,
The devil is out to sup;
But his circ' is flat,
Girl, grab your hat —
He'd *murder* to get it up!

One Hundred to One

When lawyers outnumber the teachers,
    Speeches are cheap —
      Read 'em and weep;

When soldiers outnumber the farmers,
    One hundred to one —
      Look to your gun;

When bullets outnumber the bushels,
    Swallow your fear —
      Famine is near;

When nurses outnumber survivors,
    Gather your wives —
      Flee for your lives;

When poets outnumber the preachers,
    Cast away dread —
      You're already dead.

Silly Seasons

This is the weather an editor likes,
    And so do I;
When the rag is full of gossip and strikes,
    And sales are high;
And a train derails for want of a brake,
And drunk celebrities drown in a lake,
And ministers' wives are burned at the stake,
And readers laugh 'til their bellies ache,
    And so do I.

This is the weather the editors fear,
    And so do I;
When the rag is as flat as yesterday's beer,
    And twice as dry;
And no-one has called another man 'LIAR!',
And nobody murders some lass in the choir,
And markets are quiet for seller and buyer,
And readers hurl the rag in the fire,
    And so do I!

(With apologies to Thomas Hardy.)

A Child of Adam and Eve

THERE are no 'immigrant children'
Cluttering up the land;
There is only a tyke on a beat-up bike,
Beginning to understand.

There are no 'urchin children',
Scavenging on the street;
There is only a mite in endless flight,
And never enough to eat.

There are no 'Oxfam children',
The world is grown too small;
There is only the choice — a kindly voice,
Or the shaming of us all.

There are no 'orphan children',
Whatever we may believe;
There is only this — a hug and a kiss
For a child of Adam and Eve.

Lines to the Head of His Country

I do not love you, Tony Blair,
Though this may not be fair,
And though you do not care,
I do not love you, Tony Blair.

I used to love you, Tony Blair,
When you still had your hair,
But now I'm in despair,
I used to love you, Tony Blair.

I cannot love you, Tony Blair,
Your fibs are bald and bare,
Your words are all hot air,
I cannot love you, Tony Blair.

With apologies to Thomas Brown (1663-1704)
and his famous 'Lines to the Head of His College':

I do not love you, Dr. Fell,
But why I cannot tell,
But this I know full well,
I do not love you, Dr. Fell.

Old Mother Euro

[An Everyday Story of French Farm Subsidies]

Old Mother Euro
    Went to her bureau,
To fetch her poor dog a bone;
    But when she came there
    The cupboard was bare
And so the poor dog had none.

She stumbled to Dublin
    To fetch him some ale;
But when she came back
    He was chasing his tail.

She bustled to Brussels
    To buy him a CAP,
But when she came back
    He was taking a nap.

She badgered Berliners
    To loan her a mark,
But when she came back
    He growled in the dark.

She marched to Bologna
  To fetch an umbrella;
But when she came back
  He was eating paella.

She waltzed to Vienna
  To fetch him a doctor;
But when she came back
  The silly dog mocked her.

She slipped into Paris
  To borrow a franc;
But when she came back
  He'd gone to the bank.

She limped off to Lisbon
  To fetch him some fishes;
But when she came back
  He was washing the dishes.

She went to Helsinki
  To fetch him some ice;
But when she came back
  He was dining on mice.

She paddled to London
  To fetch him some stirling;
But when she got back
  The doggy was twirling.

The dame gave a curtsy,
  The dog gave a bow;
The dame said, We're bankrupt!
  The dog said, Bow-wow.

Non!

May 29, 2005
[The French people vote 'No' to the proposed EU Constitution]

I woke to the gabble of gurus,
   Vomiting rage and fear,
Their talking-heads were bleating,
   Apocalypse was near.

"The French have shat on their masters,"
   (That's nothing new, thought I),
"And the sky above us is falling,
   Beware the falling sky!

"For without this spoon-fed tiger
   Is caged by wax and pen,
The Danes may turn to their longships,
   And the Hun may march again.

"Or the Scots shall camp at Berwick,
   And flowers of hate shall bud,
And neighbour shall war with neighbour,
   And the Tiber foam in blood.

"And the Fins may spit on Russia,
   And Spain may blaze anew,
And the Turks, Dear Lord above us,
   May riot in the queue.

"And the Dutch may fall in error,
   And the Poles may sell their vote,
And the Czechs will not stay silent
   While Yankees jeer and gloat.

"The wolves of the world are waiting
   While lambs play hide-and-seek,
And Anglo-Saxon butchers
   Work sixty hours a week.

"Here in our midst are turncoats
   Who shame our Grand Design,
And each would sell their birthright,
   For a glass of Chilean wine.

"Beware the worm-tongued meddlers,
   These johnny-come-lately crows,
Trust in the true believers
   Who shield you from their blows.

"Oh, come to your senses, children,
   And heed no siren call,
Our tariffs shall be our fortress
   Until the sky shall fall."

But the French had shat on their masters,
   (That's nothing new, thought I),
As I took my tea to the window
   To watch the falling sky.

The Numbers of the Beast

['I'm just getting on the train...']

Our lives are ruled by numbers
    That once were ruled by sin,
The slaveries of nought to nine,
  The scrambled eggs of PIN.

I walk the town— an outcast,
  I do not know my PIN,
Part heretic, part Luddite wretch,
  I text no kith or kin.

Through streets of empty chatter,
  Half-deafened by the din,
I wander in a ring-tone world,
  The no-man's-land of PIN.

Mary Had a Little Lamb

Mary had a little lamb,
His foot was black as soot,
And into Mary's bread and jam
His sooty foot he put.

Mary nabbed her little lamb
And poured herself a lager,
"If you do that again," she said,
"I'll pop you in the Aga!"

First verse from Geoffrey Wellum, leader of a
Spitfire patrol, identifying himself to base to avoid
being mistaken for a German pilot during the
Battle of Britain 1940. From his biography *First
Flight* (Penguin 2002).

55

The Diagnosis

Patronising waffle,
   Yet another test,
Traipsing through the clinic,
Stripping off my vest.

Answering their questions,
Breathing in and out,
Watching other patients
Wandering about.

Reeling off my symptoms,
Trying hard to pee,
Cursing hypodermics,
Dreading the big 'C'.

Fumbling with buttons,
Dying for a beer,
Begging the Almighty
'Get me out of here!'

Sneering at the muzak,
Leering at the nurse,
Standing for the X-rays,
Wondering which is worse —

Knowing, or not knowing.
Guzzling orangeade,
Tranquillised and dozing:
Growing more afraid.

Woken in a tizzy,
Stumbling down the hall:
"Delighted to inform you...
...nothing wrong at all."

Glory Hallelujah!
Babbling in relief;
Straight off down the boozer:
"What's your poison, chief?"

Why Do They Do It?

"I could never be a politician. I couldn't bear to
be right all the time." — Sir Peter Ustinov

Why do they do it? Why do they do it?
Why do they stand on their hind legs lying —
Lying and lying and lying and lying —
Even though everyone knows that they do it?

Even though everyone mutters: *I knew it!*
I knew it, I knew it! I <u>knew</u> they were lying!
Lying when even their mothers aren't buying.
How can they do it? How can they do it?

Spinning a web til they're lost in the thick of it,
Topping the knob til we're all of us sick of it,
Sick of the pack of 'em, spouters and stammerers,
Whining in microphones, preening for cameras,

Bullying, blaming and always denying —
And lying and lying and lying and lying.

The Grand Old Dub'ya Bush

[To the tune of 'The Grand Old Duke of York']

Oh! The Grand Old Dub'ya Bush,
  He had ten thousand men;
He marched them up to the top of Iraq
And he marched them down again.

And when there were six there were six,
And when there were four they were four,
And when there were no men left to march
He sent ten thousand more.

Oh! The Grand Old Dub'ya Bush,
He sat in a house on a hill;
He marched his men to the top of Iraq
And he has them marching still.

And when there were three there were three,
And when there was one there was one,
And when there were no men left to wack
Old Dub'ya cried; "We've won!"

Little Miss Muffet

Little Miss Muffet
Lay on a tuffet,
Her legs and her fingers entwined.

But sneaky Jack Horner
Crept out from a corner
To warn her, "It makes you go blind!"

Perhaps

'How came the walls to tumble?
          How came the roof to fall?
How came the girders flying
          To crush and kill us all?'

We built with solid mortar,
          The walls were up to spec',
Perhaps the earth turned traitor
          And slippage caused the wreck?

'How came the train to carnage,
          The metal points to stall?
How came the rails to buckle
          To crush and kill us all?'

We built as per the blueprint,
          The track was up to spec'.
Perhaps a signal failure
          Or vandals caused the wreck?

'How came the crowded ferry
To roll beyond recall?
How came the rotten lifeboats
To sink and drown us all?'

The boats were built to order,
The ship was up to spec'.
Perhaps uncharted breakers
Or panic caused the wreck?

*

'Perhaps when you must join us,
Your corpses in the sod,
You'll find your reinsurance
Won't cover Acts of God.'

Old Osama Had a Farm

Old Osama had a farm, E I E I O;
And on his farm he had some men, E I E I O;
With a brain wash here and a brain wash there,
Here a brain, there a wash, everywhere a brain wash.
Old Osama had a farm, E I E I O.

Old Osama had a cave, E I E I O;
And in his cave he had some guns, E I E I O;
With a flash bang here and a flash bang there,
Here a flash, there a bang, everywhere a flash bang.
Old Osama had a cave, E I E I O.

Old Osama had a camp, E I E I O;
And in his camp he had some bombs, E I E I O;
With a boom boom here and a boom boom there,
Here a boom, there a boom, everywhere a boom boom.
Old Osama had a camp, E I E I O.

Fools

"Mit der Dummheit kampfein Götter selbst vergebens."
— Schiller The Maid of Orleans

Fools, fools, fools:
In our factories, cities and schools,
The dunces and duffers,
The boobies and bluffers...
We'll never be free of the fools.

Our shops and our hospitals littered
With fatheaded asses to pay;
We dare not annoy them,
We're forced to employ them —
They cost more to keep locked away.

Fools, fools, fools:
Perhaps you know some who know you?
But once you start counting
The total keeps mounting,
It's scary, but what can you do?

I hear they are running the country,
I *know* they are driving this bus;
We're helpless and hounded,
They've got us surrounded —
There's far more of them than of us!

Fools, fools fools:
> *They rule us by day and by night;*
>> *We dance to their rhythm,*
>> *No arguing with 'em...*
> *They're always so certain they're right.*

The surgeon who saws a wrong limb off;
> The plumber who 'knows what he's worth';
>> The bodgers in trainers,
>> The 'mustn't complain'ers' —
> They cover the face of the earth.

Fools, fools, fools:
> *With their doltish and cretinous rules;*
>> *The sad diagnosis?*
>> *They breed by osmosis...*
> *And we'll never be free of the fools...*

No, we'll <u>never</u> be free of the Fools!

"Roll Up! Roll Up!"

Life is a terminal bungle,
Whatever you do: no-win.
We live in a zoo, in a jungle,
Where the tigers are breaking *in*.

Life's an impossible circus,
The cavalry never arrive;
By accident — or on purpose,
No-one gets out alive.

Rub-a-dub-dub

[A G8 jingle]

Rub-a-dub-dub, eight men in a club
Have gathered from over the sea,
    They talk of Free Trade
    And the progress they've made,
Though *free* trade is never quite *free*.

Rub-a-dub-dub, and here is the nub,
Your leaders may waffle and jaw,
    But goods stay protected
    To keep them elected,
While we stay as poor as before.

Rub-a-dub-dub, you men in your club,
Whose speeches are crafted with care,
    If aid merely caters
    To rotten dictators—
Then spare us, at least, the hot air.

Telling Lies

All the angels up in heaven
   Hang their shining heads to cry;
Even Santa Claus grows solemn
   When you tell your mum a lie.

And the fairies in the garden
   Who leave silver for your tooth,
They will whisper, if you ask them:
   "Always tell your mum the truth".

If you don't believe in fairies,
   Or that reindeer ever flew,
You might murmur three Hail Mary's
   For the lies your mum told you.

'Hush-a-bye, baby...'

Hush-a-bye, baby, on the tree top,
When the wind blows the cradle will rock;
When the Bundesbank orders the Euro to fall,
Down will come baby, cradle and all.

The Effects of Sex

To gauge the effects of the demon sex
Expunge all froth and lathers,
And turn thine eyes from prudish lies,
O child of a thousand fathers!

Adam'n'Eve could scarce believe
    Jehovah's righteous passion;
And bit, to boot, forbidden fruit —
Thus fig leaves led to fashion.

Bathed in milk and decked in silk,
Queen Cleopatra's fascia
Enraptured Caesar, who, to please her
Slaughtered half of Asia.

Helen of Troy and a big, tall boy
Called Paris, fled like silly 'uns.
Gorgeous hips, a thousand ships
And the Trojans died in millions.

Delilah lopped off Samson's mop,
Post coitus, in a saucer.
For one great night that Israelite
Near lost the Philistine war, sir!

Napoleon's Queen, fair Josephine,
Once begged him not to touch her.
Deprived of this pneumatic bliss
The fool invaded Russia.

Madam Mao was a cunning cow
In search of her own salvation;
She bent the plan of a sad old man
And crucified her nation.

Norma Jean had a fatal scene
With Kennedy as her lover;
(Though sadly dead, I've heard it said
She also knew his brother).

John met Yoko, then went loco
Bellowing 'Primal Foetals!'
Ono droned, the fans all moaned,
And *that* was the end of The Beatles.

Princess Di' was young and shy,
The nations all assembled
To watch her wed, but the magic fled
And the House of Windsor trembled.

Young Jack and Jill still climb the hill
And it's not <u>that</u> complex, sir.
If you would sleuth for history's truth...
Just check the effects of <u>sex</u>, sir!

The Ballad of 'Abdul' Rowe

I tell of a teacher, Abdul Rowe,
Who taught— not so many years ago—
In Northwood Hills, at a grammar school,
Where he changed the life of a callow fool.

Thank you, Abdul, thank you!
You looked a proper tyro —
We thought you weird
With your big black beard
And a multi-purpose biro.

It was back in nineteen sixty-three,
And I was the king of form 4C,
A vipers tongue and last in class,
Lord, how the prefects whacked my arse!

Thank you, Abdul, thank you!
We may have been unruly,
And pinned a note
On the back of your coat,
I apologise, Abdul, truly.

In those days I was a mouthy lout
With precious little to mouth about,
I kept the bullies off my back
By feeding masters cheek and flack.

Thank you, Abdul, thank you!
Forgive that little tartar
Who brought you fame,
A sly nickname,
And turned you into a martyr.

Now Abdul Rowe was a substitute
On English Lit', a new recruit,
A softy, wet behind the ears —
(I knew we'd soon have him in tears).

Thank you, Abdul thank you!
You didn't rant or rave, sir.
You didn't shout
Or bang us about
To force us to behave, sir.

He dressed far worse than any boy,
His suits were shabby corduroy,
He couldn't discipline a fly
(And he knew it, too, so he didn't try).

Thank you, Abdul, thank you!
We howled like drunk carousers,
(Yes, it was me
And Johnny P
Who superglued your trousers.)

Through all this riot that poor saint
Would smile and never make complaint,
Until one day, out loud, he made
Us read *The Charge of the Light Brigade*.

Thank you, Abdul, thank you!
He read like a transformed giant!
He struck 4C's
Artillery,
And the class became compliant.

He knew he'd hooked us then, by God!
And sure enough he cast a rod
Across that lake of clueless proles,
And reeled in a few stray souls.

Thank you, Abdul, thank you!
You won't recall those scholars.
You never knew —
But it was you
Who made me a million dollars!

Envoi: Thank you, Abdul, thank you!
By God, I wish you well, sir,
And as you'll note
From what I've wrote,
I've half-way learned to spell, sir!

There really was an 'Abdul' Rowe (whose first name I never did learn) at St. Nicholas Grammar School in the early 1960's. And he really did change my life, although neither of us could have known it at the time. He once wrote in my exercise book beside an essay: "If you keep this up, Dennis, we'll have you in a green-backed Penguin yet!" Forty years later, I still remember those words. The carrot is mightier than the stick! And, by God, we had plenty of stick!

Winning the Lottery

"Lid it, laddie! Just a minute!
        Lemme 'ear the draw, my son.
'Course we're never gonna win it,
        Every week I bloody bin it,
Still, you gotta try it, innit?
...*Christ Almighty, son! We've won!*"

Dad goes mental! Mum rejoices!
        Here comes spongers by the ton.
Snotty lawyers, endless choices,
        Jealous relatives, raised voices,
Aston Martins and Rolls Royces
...Villas in the Spanish sun.

Laddie meets a Page 3 slapper,
        (Marriage photo in *The Sun*),
Daughter dates a hip-hop rapper
        Graduates Phi Beta Kappa,
Gives birth to a whipper-snapper
...Laddie does a hit and run.

Dad goes mental! Mum gets tearful.
        (Yet *more* pictures in *The Sun*).
Daughter gets a bleedin' earful,
        Laddie's Q.C. growing fearful
See's no reason to be cheerful
...Thinks he'll go down, ten to one.

Daughter turning anorexic,
(Yet *more* pictures in *The Sun*).
Laddie steals a car and wrecks it,
Page 3 slapper makes her exit,
Mum meets gigolo and necks it,
... "Jesus wept, wot 'ave I done?"

* * *

"Wake up Dad and stop that racket!
Mum? She's gone to buy *The Sun*.
Have you seen my leather jacket?
Wrote me numbers on a packet.
'Course, I know we'll never crack it.
...Be a larf, though, if we won!"

'There was a Mao Zedong...'

There was a Mao Zedong, and he had a little gun,
And his bullets were made of lead, lead, lead;
And he won a lot of wars, and wrote a lot of laws,
But his citizens were barely getting fed, fed, fed.

He gathered new recruits, who hadn't any boots,
And the colour of his Guards was red, red, red;
Then he chided them to cheer his clever new idea
To harrow every field sparrow dead, dead, dead.

"For sparrows eat the seed our hungry peasants need,
Go and kill them all," is what he said, said, said;
They parroted his words, and murdered all the birds,
And made a pigeon pie and went to bed, bed, bed.

So many sparrows died, the insects multiplied,
And famine came to visit as they bred, bred, bred;
Then Helmsman Mao Zedong took his nasty little gun,
And shot a lot of traitors in the head, head, head.

Chairman Mao Zedong's 'Great Leap Forward' in the late 1950's helped to kill more than 20 million Chinese peasants in the famine that followed. Part of his plan demanded that all the sparrows and other seed-eating birds in China be exterminated to reduce crop losses. The results were catastrophic — and not just for the sparrows. Truly, folly wreaks more havoc than malice.

TV Dinners

This talking head is:'Quote, unquote:
A testament to dental art'—
Let's slip a skewer down its throat
And snack upon its shrivelled heart.

The Politician

The late night news, all wit and charm,
Here's every viewer's trusted friend —
What say we both yank off an arm
And marinade the sticky end?

The Newsreader

Here's Martha Stewart, hip hurrah,
Who's still the queen of cookery —
Let's shred her into steak tartar
And scoff it while we watch TV.

The Celebrity Homemaker

That rotter Dick has jilted Sasch'
For some young tart— I knew he would,
A slice-and-dice will fix their hash:
Say mad-cow roast and cheesecake pud?

Soap Opera Stars

A rerun of the Superbowl!
Fresh booby pie with steroid sauce —
On second thoughts —a casserole!
And pompoms for the second course!

The Sports Commentator

Old Mickey Mouse on Medicare,
Long past his prime, I'll pass on that —
It's not exactly gourmet fare,
He's barely fit to feed the cat.

The Cartoon

At last, it's Oprah!   Fetch the bibs,
The charcoal grill, the mesquite wood —
There nothing spare about those ribs,
She'll feed the whole damn neighbourhood!

The Chat Show Diva

Old Fart

Certain that all rap is crap,
　　Its assonance an utter bore,
Wishing I could gangsta slap
That face beneath its woolly cap...

Yet sensing slowing in the sap
　　From 1 who sampled youth be4,
I settle puss upon my lap,
　　And call myself a dinosaur...

For thO I *think* all rap is crap,
　　(Self-consciousness its f8tal flaw),
I nurse a K9 handicap:
　　Young dogs grows rich —
　　　　　　Old farts stay poor.

The House That Crack Built

This is the pipe
That lay in the house that crack built.

This is the puff,
That filled the pipe
That lay in the house that crack built.

This is the stuff,
That would not puff,
That filled the pipe
That lay in the house that crack built.

This is the sod,
That sold the stuff,
That would not puff,
That filled the pipe
That lay in the house that crack built.

This is the gun with the barrel sawn,
That shot the sod,
That sold the stuff,
That would not puff,
That filled the pipe
That lay in the house that crack built.

This is the room with the curtains drawn
That hid the gun with the barrel sawn,
That shot the sod,
That sold the stuff,
That would not puff,
That filled the pipe
That lay in the house that crack built.

This is the man who slept at dawn,
That lived in the room with the curtains drawn,
That sold the gun with the barrel sawn,
That shot the sod,
That sold the stuff,
That would not puff,
That filled the pipe
That lay in the house that crack built.

This is the frock all tattered and torn,
That kept the man who slept at dawn,
That lived in the room with the curtains drawn,
That sold the gun with the barrel sawn,
That shot the sod,
That sold the stuff,
That would not puff,
That filled the pipe
That lay in the house that crack built.

This is the maiden all forlorn,
That wore the frock all tattered and torn,
That kept the man who slept at dawn,
That lived in the room with the curtains drawn,
That sold the gun with the barrel sawn,
That shot the sod,
That sold the stuff,
That would not puff,
That filled the pipe
That lay in the house that crack built.

This is the babe that never was born,
That died in the womb of a maid forlorn,
That wore the frock all tattered and torn,
That kept the man who slept at dawn,
That lived in the room with the curtains drawn,
That sold the gun with the barrel sawn,
That shot the sod,
That sold the stuff,
That would not puff,
That filled the pipe
That lay in the house that crack built.

Nebuchadnezzar

Nebuchadnezzar
    was taking his pleasure,
Rocking at leisure
    while sipping his wine.
"Dost thou grow tired
    of love thou hast hired?"
Politely enquired
    his young concubine.

"Abigail, truly,
    thy tongue grows unruly!
Am I not duly
    the sire of thy heart?"
"If thou would know it
    Command! I must show it,
Yet the worth of a poet
    is all in his art!"

Turning to trail
    the hem of her veil,
Sweet Abigail
    died there on the swings.
Never tease lions
    with open defiance.
Place no reliance
    on princes or kings.

Do ye ken John Peel

[for John Peel, British disc jockey – 1939-2004]

Do ye ken John Peel
    with his coat so gay?
Do ye ken John Peel
    now he's upped and away?
Do ye ken John Peel—
    he's a grand DJ
On the BBC
in the evening?

Did ye ken John Peel
    when he played Top Gear?
Did ye ken John Peel
    with his Gandalf's ear?
Did ye ken John Peel
    play the Pistols, dear, —
On the BBC
in the evening?

Did ye ken John Peel
    with his T-Rex bones?
Did ye ken John Peel
    and the Undertones?
Did ye ken John Peel?
    How he loved unknowns!
On the BBC
in the evening?

Did ye ken John Peel?
  (Oh, he'd hate the fuss)
Did ye ken John Peel
  on the Magic Bus?
Did ye ken John Peel?
  He was one of us
On the BBC
in the evening.

Did ye ken John Peel
  when his hair was grey?
Do you ken John Peel
  now he's far, far away?
Do ye ken John Peel
  Now there's no-one to play
On the BBC
in the evening?

Falling, falling
[September 11, 2001]

Mommy! Mommy! Come and see!
The lady says it's history
Falling on 'hew-man-ity'.
Mommy! Mommy! Come and see!

All the world is calling, calling;
All the world is falling, falling...

Mommy! Mommy! Please don't cry.
Things are falling from the sky,
Look! A man has learned to fly!
Mommy! Mommy! Please don't cry.

All the world is calling, calling;
All the world is falling, falling...

Mommy, who was that who called?
See where all the smoke has crawled!
Mommy! Look! The tower has falled!
Mommy, who was that who called?

All the world is calling, calling;
All the world is falling,
f
a
l
l
i
n
g

Tony Blair and his Merry Men

[to the tune of Robin Hood]

Tony Blair, Tony Blair
  Riding through the glen;
Tony Blair, Tony Blair
  With his band of men;
Longs to be loved,
  Life isn't fair —
Tony Blair, Tony Blair, Tony Blair.

Friar John, Friar John
  Driving in his Jag;
Friar John, Friar John
  Peerage in the bag;
Hooks like a duck,
  Thinks he's a swan —
Friar John, Friar John, Friar John.

Gordon Brown, Gordon Brown
  Dying to take charge;
Gordon Brown, Gordon Brown
  Prince of sabotage;
Brown's going green
  Robbed of the crown —
Gordon Brown, Gordon Brown, Gordon Brown.

Mandel-son, Mandel-son
  God of little things;
Mandel-son, Mandel-son
  Sulking in the wings;
Knows he'll be back,
  Watch Mandy run!
Mandel-son, Mandel-son, Mandel-son.

Tony Blair, Tony Blair
  Master of the spin;
Tony Blair, Tony Blair
  With his silly grin;
Does Tony care?
  Ask Alistair!
Tony Blair, Tony Blair, Tony Blair.

The True Interpretation of American Signs and Announcements

THANK YOU FOR NOT SMOKING
(...if I've quit so can you);

TIPPING IS PERMITTED
(...cash is fine);

FOR YOUR OWN PROTECTION
(...it's peanuts if you sue);

YOUR CALL'S IMPORTANT TO US
(...wait on line).

STRICTLY MEMBERS ONLY
(...we've tested it in court);

SAFETY IS OUR MOTTO
(...don't you dare!)

PLEASE CONSULT YOUR MANUAL
(...no one home at tech' support);

TELL ME HOW I'M DRIVING
(...like I care).

THANK YOU FOR YOUR PATIENCE
(...Mastercard or Visa?)

MISSING YOU ALREADY
(...have they gone?)

DRIVER IS ALLERGIC
(...but not to garlic pizza);

YOU HAVE WON A MILLION DOLLARS!
(...dream on!)

The Troubles

As I was passing Dublin Gate,
I met a man who dined on hate,
Who supped upon a sea of song
Made bitter by an ancient wrong.

As I passed through a Belfast mist,
I met a man who shook his fist,
Who preyed upon the men of hate
Who crept at night through Dublin Gate.

As I was passing Cromwell Street,
I met a man blown off his feet,
Who scrawled in blood upon a stone:
No prisoners! God will know His own!

As I was passing Parliament,
I met a man whose orders sent
Young squaddies out upon the street
To shoot at men they'd never meet.

As I was passing New York State,
I met a man who heaped a plate
With others' pain— who paid a fee
To be a part of 'history'.

As I passed by a widow's door,
I heard a cry: *"Dear Christ, no more!*
A pox upon your Dublin Gate,
Your Belfast mist... your men of hate."

Pillow Talk

"Mother, he loves me— and yet I fear
That love is *unresolved*
When marriage is omitted."

"Think, then, of bacon and eggs, my dear.
The chicken is *involved;*
The porker is *committed!*"

Acknowledgements

I have collected many volumes of nursery rhymes over the years, but for the writing of this book I came back again and again to *The Oxford Dictionary of Nursery Rhymes* by Iona and Peter Opie (OUP), and to an edition of *The Nursery Rhymes of England* by James Orchard Halliwell. These were my main sources for original rhymes and street ballads. I heartily recommend them as treasure troves of antiquity and edification, where, for example, readers may learn of the singer, Mrs. Buzgago, whose favourite song on stage was:

> See-saw, Margery Daw,
> Sold her bed and lay upon straw;
> Sold her bed and lay upon hay
> And pisky came and carried her away.
> For wasn't she a dirty slut
> To sell her bed and lie upon dirt.

I wish to thank the following people for help in the production of this book: Caroline Rush who patiently shepherded it through its many incarnations; Simon Rae and Moni Manning who advised on selection; Dana Gillespie and Alan Marcuson for a couple of word-play gems; George Taylor and Harvey Brough and all the children involved in the production of the CD; the team at Ebury Press and Random House; Sebastian Krueger and Bill Sanderson for their terrific illustrations and Mike Dunn for his imperturbable design and colouring work.

Those wishing to see Bill's and Sebastian's illustrations in wide-screen, digital glory will find them at *www.felixdennis.com*